Dear Lyndon, Rosanna & Kids:

Wishing you all had a memorable trip to Houston. Many Blessings!

Wayne, Aijun, Aaron, Joshua & Grace

July '2001

HOUSTON, TEXAS

A PHOTOGRAPHIC PORTRAIT

PHOTOGRAPHY BY JIM OLIVE

First published in the United States
of America by:

Twin Lights Publishers, Inc.
8 Hale Street
Rockport, Massachusetts 01966
Telephone: (978) 546-7398
http://www.twinlightspub.com

ISBN: 1-885435-68-1
ISBN: 978-1885435-68-2

10 9 8 7 6 5 4 3

TEXAS BLUE BONNETS *(right)*

Named for its color and the
resemblance of its petal to a
woman's sunbonnet, the Texas
Blue Bonnet is the state flower.
Blooming in early spring, it's
found all over central and
south Texas.

Editorial researched and written by
Francesca and Duncan Yates

Book design by
SYP Design & Production, Inc.
http://www.sypdesign.com

Printed in China

Welcome to Houston...
the Big City on the Buffalo Bayou

I n an 1837 advertisment, the Allen brothers, Augustus and John, proclaimed: *"This town will become the great, interior, commercial emporium of Texas... ships from New York and Paris will sail to our door. They'll be continual sea breezes from the Gulf."*

Well, the ships didn't sail. The breezes didn't blow. And the swamps backed up. That same year, the Houston census was twelve people huddled in one log cabin. It is history, however, that usually decides who had a vision of the future and who had an aversion to it. The Allen brothers had a vision, and they named it *Houston*.

When the Lucas Gusher blew at Spindletop in 1901, Texas changed forever. By 1929, forty oil companies had offices in Houston and refineries along the Houston Ship Channel, safe from Gulf storms. The oil gushed for eighty years and transformed Houston into one of the richest cities in the world.

Throughout the pages of this photographic portrait, award-winning photographer Jim Olive presents powerful images of this culturally vibrant city on the bayou, where history is now being made in the fields of medicine, cancer research, higher education, space exploration, cargo shipping, agriculture and environmental awareness.

The vast wealth from petroleum, cattle and shipping that has made Houston the fourth largest city in America is remaking Houston today. Houston is not only a wealthy city, it's a wiser one. A city of which the Allen brothers would be proud.

DOWNTOWN HOUSTON *(opposite)*

Formerly home to the Enron Corporation, these two skyscrapers are joined by a distinctive circular skyway. In the blazing Texas sun, the blue glass of the 50-story tower on the left reflects light in all directions.

BUFFALO BAYOU *(above)*

Houston was built on the south bank of
Buffalo Bayou at its junction with White
Oak Bayou. A wild, flowing landscape
through Houston, this 52-mile river is a
refreshing escape from the heat and fast
pace of city life.

SAM HOUSTON PARK *(opposite)*

In 1900, this land, then on the edge of town,
became Houston's first public park and is
still the city's premier green space. The
Museum of Texas History is located here,
along with several faithfully restored struc-
tures, including a cabin and a church.

MECOM FOUNTAIN *(above)*

One of Houston's oldest parks, Hermann Park is home to the city's finest cultural and recreational attractions, including a zoo, natural science museum, planetarium, arts museum, outdoor theatre, gardens and fountains.

WORTHAM CENTER *(opposite)*

Located in Houston's acclaimed Theater District, the center is home to the city's opera, ballet and two theater companies. Houston is one of five U.S. cities with professional companies for opera, ballet, music, and theater.

BAYOU BEND COLLECTION AND GARDENS *(above and opposite)*

Experience the elegant lifestyle of the early 20th century in the breathtaking nationally-acclaimed gardens and former home of noted Houston philanthropist and collector Ima Hogg. Her mansion at Bayou Bend presently contains several thousand objects in period room settings that showcase American decorative arts from 1620 through 1870. Miss Hogg donated the mansion, property, and art collections to Houston's Museum of Fine Arts.

BUFFALO BAYOU PROMANADE

A walkway follows the curves of Buffalo Bayou, Houston's stately, slow-moving river, on its journey through downtown. This picturesque promenade meanders through twenty-three acres of new parks, filled with artwork, native landscaping, and dramatic moon-friendly lights that change from electric blue to white in sync with the cycles of the moon. The undersides of many bridges passing over the bayou now have a cobalt glow.

MEMORIAL PARK GOLF COURSE *(above)*

This golf course was originally built in 1923 for soldiers who were patients at the Army hospital at Camp Logan. After the hospital closed, the nine-hole course was re-designed for eighteen holes and opened to the public.

TOUR 18 GOLF COURSE *(opposite)*

Imagine being able to play the best holes of America's greatest golf courses in one day. Replicas of 18 legendary course holes challenge brave and fearless golfers at this one-of-a-kind public golf course. Be sure to bring your best game.

SAN JACINTO MONUMENT

The San Jacinto Monument marks a site as
synonymous with Texas as the Alamo; it is
the famous battleground where General Sam
Houston's troops won Texas' independence
from Mexico in 1836 against the infamous
General Santa Ana.

HOUSTON CENTER FOUNTAIN

Developed in the heart of the city's dynamic business district, the Houston Center is a multi-use real estate complex. Adjacent to the convention center, it features upscale hotels, apartments, fine dining, and Houston's only downtown shopping mall.

ANTIOCH MISSIONARY BAPTIST
CHURCH *(above)*

Overshadowed by skyscrapers, this little brick
church was organized and built in 1875 by
former slaves. As the first house of worship
owned by African Americans in Houston, it
remains a proud symbol of Black heritage.

NIELS ESPERSON BUIDING *(opposite)*

This jewel in the crown of Houston's downtown is a classic example of Italian Renaissance architecture. When the building is lit at
night, its columns, urns, terraces and grand
tempietto can be viewed at great distances.

VIEW FROM SPOT PARK *(opposite)*

Houston's towering skyline dwarfs a nearby residential community, reminding us of the phenomenal growth this Gulf Coast city has experienced since the Lucas Gusher at Spindletop gave birth to the oil industry in 1901.

M.D. ANDERSON CANCER CENTER *(top)*

Located at Houston's famous Texas Medical Center, the world's largest medical complex, the M.D. Anderson Cancer Center was ranked thirteenth in the nation by *U.S. News & World Report* and treats 70,000 patients annually.

HOUSTON AERIAL *(bottom)*

Traffic whips around the perimeter of Houston's downtown in a red blur of tail lights, symbolizing her rapid growth. Now the fourth largest city in America, the influence of Houston's resources and production are recognized globally.

ROOT MEMORIAL PARK *(above)*

This aging downtown park recently enjoyed a
$2.3 million makeover with the hope that it
would become a popular venue for top-shelf
street basketball. Surrounded by sculptures
and lovely gardens, the new court provides
tiered seating that is shaded by oak trees.

WORTHAM CENTER *(opposite)*

Covering two city blocks, the performing arts
center hosts the Houston Ballet, Houston
Grand Opera and Theater Under the Stars.
It is a stunning building with high ceilings,
a grandiose, multi-terraced foyer and spectacular city views.

LIGHT RAIL *(opposite and above)*

The sleek and modern cars of Houston's new Light Rail system have quickly become a familiar sight around the city; however, there was a time when the controversial project had few supporters. After Light Rail's success in Dallas in 1996, Houston embraced the new system. Today trains arrive every 12 minutes throughout a 19-hour day. The sprawling, mile-long Texas Medical Center in South Houston is the line's most prominent destination.

THE WATER WALL *(above)*

This city landmark, on the campus of the Houston Medical Center, is a cool oasis for visitors. The spectacular, 64-foot-high urban waterfall drops thousands of gallons every minute, bringing texture, sound, and visual interest to a simple concrete facade.

MARKET SQUARE CLOCK TOWER *(opposite)*

Commissioned in 1904, this historic Seth Thomas clock was originally in a bell tower at Houston's City Hall at Market Square. Packed away and misplaced for over eighty years, the clock and bell were finally reunited in 1996.

OPTI RACING ON CLEAR LAKE

Adolescents have many opportunities to hone
their sailing skills on the waterways around
Houston, culminating in the annual Texas
Youth Race Week. Here young sailors
maneuver their Optimist dinghies toward
the finish line.

LUXURY CRUISE PORT OF CALL

Even though Houston has been one of the world's largest ports for decades, it was not a port of call for cruise ships until 1997. With thirty-one million people within a 500-mile radius, luxury ships' arrivals and departures are now a common sight.

UNIVERSITY OF HOUSTON

(above and opposite)

With over 35,000 students, UH is the third-largest university in Texas and the only one with doctoral degree programs. Located on a 560-acre campus southeast of downtown Houston, it operates more than forty research centers and institutes on campus. Faculty includes Pulitzer Prize winner Edward Albee, National Medal of Science winner Paul Chu and Nobel Peace Prize Laureate and recipient Jody Williams.

NIELS ESPERSON BUILDING

An urn is one of the many elaborate details
incorporated into the design of this Italian
Renaissance building. At 32 stories, it was
the tallest in Texas when it opened in 1927 as
a tribute to real estate and oil millionaire
Niels Esperson by his widow.

SABINE STREET BRIDGE

This scenic pedestrian bridge crosses over
Buffalo Bayou Park, Houston's expansive
greenway along the banks of Buffalo Bayou.
The downtown bridge is the site of a
constantly changing collection of delightful
public art works.

HOLIDAY SPIRIT

Houston celebrates the beginning of the holiday season by lighting a 45-foot tree in
Hermann Square Park at City Hall. A tour
of other downtown decorations includes
lighted trains, a herd of grazing reindeer, toy
soldiers, and a forest of lighted trees.

BAYOU PLACE

This ambitious entertainment complex, in the heart of Houston's popular Theater District, features great pubs, billiards, restaurants, multiplex theaters, art house films and concert halls, all under one roof.

36

MAIN STREET SQUARE *(opposite)*

Main Street Square is Houston's new downtown, central plaza. A hallmark of great cities, the car-free plaza features innovative architecture, dramatic water fountains, landscaping, shops, public art and two stations of the new Light Rail system.

METRO TROLLY *(above)*

The mile-long campus of the world-renowned Texas Medical Center is easy to get around, thanks to METRO's special TMC trolley. Employees, visitors and students can hop aboard at frequent campus stops between 6 AM and 6 PM.

GALLERIA ICE SKATING RINK (top)

Shoppers can take a break, strap on their
skates and cut some figure eights at the ice
skating rink that is located at the center of
Houston's Galleria Mall. Private lessons are
also available.

LIGHT RAIL FOUNTAIN (bottom)

Houston's new Light Rail system was designed
to be a convenient and attractive addition to
the cityscape. The tracks are landscaped with
colorful flower borders and dramatic water
fountains that arch high over the tracks.

POWER OF HOUSTON LIGHT SHOW

Each year, over 150 blocks of downtown
Houston play host to a much-heralded fire-
works, laser-light, and music extravaganza.
Sponsored by Reliant Energy, the thirty-
minute program highlights a three-day city-
wide festival. Special effects experts use a
jaw-dropping 50,000 pounds of explosives.

RIVER OAKS *(opposite, top and bottom)*

River Oaks is an exclusive urban community developed within the heart of Houston in 1920. A neighborhood of big trees, big names and big money, its upscale homes and resplendent mansions sell for anywhere from $1 million to $20 million.

MIDTOWN *(above)*

In the 1980s, Midtown was home to "Little Saigon," a Vietnamese neighborhood and cultural center. Today Midtown keeps the night lights burning with trendy clubs, restaurants, bars, theatres, shops and art galleries.

MEMORIAL PARK

Dubbed "the largest urban park in Texas," Memorial Park covers over 1,400 green acres inside the Loop 610 highway. It offers visitors a top-ranked golf course, jogging trails, and venues for swimming, tennis, and softball, to name just a few.

MORMON TEMPLE OF HOUSTON

This grand Mormon Temple comprised of
shimmering luna pearl granite in northwest
Houston, serves a community of 83,000
Latter-Day Saints. A tall spire rises up from
the 34,000-square-foot structure with a gold-
en sculpture of the angel, Moroni, at its apex.

RICE UNIVERSITY *(top and bottom)*

When Houston philanthropist William Marsh Rice was killed by his greedy valet in 1900, Rice's carefully laid plans for creating a top-notch university were nearly sabotaged. An autopsy exposed the murder, and the city of Houston was free to implement Rice's dream of a private, independent university. Today the campus of internationally acclaimed Rice University covers 300 acres near the downtown area and rivals the reputations of Ivy League universities back east.

CITY HALL *(opposite)*

"Here in America, we are rapidly developing our own type of architecture," Joseph Finger declared in 1937 in defense of his then-ultra-modern, design for the new City Hall. *"We are building for the masses, not the classes."*

BAYOU BEND

The grounds surrounding this branch of the
Museum of Fine Arts include eight formal
gardens of azaleas, gardenias, antique roses,
rare, pink camellias, magnolias and crepe
myrtles, alongside animal-shaped topiaries
and goddess statuary.

COCKRELL BUTTERFLY CENTER

One of the most visited museums in the country, the Houston Museum of Natural Science, is a five-venue complex housing a Dome Theatre, IMAX Theatre, The Cockrell Butterfly Center and four floors of natural science halls and exhibits. On the first floor, hands-on exhibits at Fondren Discovery Place delight kids and adults. Inside the three-story Butterfly Center is a naturalistic rainforest showcasing hundreds of live butterflies. Creepy crawly bugs can be seen at the center's Insect Zoo.

MUSEUM OF FINE ARTS *(opposite)*

Considered by many to be the best public art museum in Texas, Houston's Museum of Fine Arts features a prolific collection of over 40,000 works of art from cultures around the world.

MUSEUM OF NATURAL SCIENCE *(above)*

From tiny insects to the largest animals to ever walk the earth, this museum hosts a spectacular variety of internationally acclaimed exhibits, including the finest collection of gems and minerals in the world.

JOHN P. MCGOVERN
CHILDREN'S ZOO

A family favorite, the John P. McGovern
Children's Zoo provides kids of all ages a
hands-on experience while making friends
with animals.

WATERWHEEL

Children flock to the zoo's water park, a refreshing playground in a coastal fishing village setting with features such as pop jets and foaming fountains. Behind the scenes, a computer sets off streams of water in random patterns, while children delight in the unexpected fun.

"VIRTUOSO," LYRIC CENTER *(left)*

It's almost impossible for Houston sculptor David Adickes to think small. He is well known for his gigantic statues, such as this cello, and a 67-foot-tall statue of beloved Texas hero, Sam Houston. The downtown area includes a wealth of such public artworks.

SAM HOUSTON EXHIBIT *(right)*

This bronze statue of Sam Houston greets those entering City Hall's new state-of-the-art Visitors Center. The new center, part of major renovations to the landmark civic building, features a variety of museum-quality historical displays.

THE HOUSTON SYMPHONY

Hans Graff conducts the widely-acclaimed Houston Symphony. One of the top orchestras in the world, the symphony performs more than 170 concerts each year. The accomplished musicians also volunteer as soloists and music coaches throughout Houston.

GRAND FOYER *(top and opposite)*

Wortham Center's six-story Grand Foyer provides an elegant and impressive setting for hosting a variety of civic gatherings and social galas. From a mezzanine above, visitors view stunning sculptures by Albert Paley and a view of the adjacent plaza.

MILLER OUTDOOR THEATRE *(bottom)*

The Miller Outdoor Theatre provides free shows, many of which are full productions of the same musicals, plays and operas performed at Houston's indoor theaters. This delightful performance space is located in Hermann Park, near the zoo.

HOUSTON INTERNATIONAL
FESTIVAL *(above)*

A moment of colorful solitude is captured
at this beloved spring festival. One million
visitors come to enjoy world-class musical
performances, international foods, and
unique treasures from around the globe.

AQUARIUM RESTAURANT
FOUNTAIN *(opposite)*

The star-shaped spouts of this playful fountain are just one of the fun attractions at this
aquarium/restaurant/amusement park complex. The fish are not only on the menu, but
are all around in large and small aquariums.

CLEAR LAKE *(above)*

Clear Lake is the third-largest pleasure boat basin in the United States. Yachts, sporting boats and fishing vessels fill its 9,000 marina slips, while its many lakeside communities enjoy refreshing Gulf breezes year-round.

ORANGE SHOW *(opposite)*

The Orange Show began as a retired Postman's personal, avant-garde celebration of the health benefits of oranges. Today Houston's popular Orange Show has grown to be one of the most important folk-art expositions in the country.

ART CAR PARADE, ORANGE SHOW
(top and bottom)

The parade draws hundreds of thousands of
folk-art enthusiasts every year, all eager to
view the most audacious and glittering assem-
blage of auto art ever created.

KEMAH BOARDWALK *(opposite)*

Twenty miles from Houston, you can enjoy
the famous breezes from Galveston Bay at
Kemah's Boardwalk, a popular, waterfront
experience with fun-park rides for kids and
mouth-watering restaurants for adults.

HOUSTON MARATHON *(top)*

For over thirty years, the Houston Marathon has been a favorite on the U.S. runners' tour. It is often called the best kept secret in U.S. marathons. Now, with close to one million dollars in prizes, the secret is officially out.

TEXACO GRAND PRIX *(above and opposite)*

Houston loves fast cars, as the roar of the crowds will tell you. Grand Prix combines three days and nights of racing at Reliant Park, featuring American Le Mans sports cars and technological marvels known as *Champ* cars.

HOUSTON INTERNATIONAL FESTIVAL

This city-wide festival is one of Houston's largest events, drawing more than one million visitors over two weeks in April. The festival features juried arts, crafts, food, music, games and cultural events for all ages.

CINCO DE MAYO *(top and bottom)*

The Cinco de Mayo Festival originally cele-
brated a single, surprising win by Mexicans
over the army of an occupying French force
on May 5, 1862. The festival has grown to
symbolize national pride and the triumph
over foreign occupation.

RENAISSANCE FESTIVAL

Share a day of medieval revelry with friends
and family at the Texas Renaissance Festival
in Plantersville. After thirty-two years,
Houston knows how to *get medieval*. Visitors
experience the fashions, customs, crafts, skills
and leisure activities of this bygone era.

JOUSTING COMPETITION

A favorite among many patrons to the festival is the jousting tournament, which takes place daily in the tournament field. The king and queen, along with other lords and ladies, cheer for their favorite knight to win and be crowned the "royal champion."

ALABAMA-COUSHATTA TRIBE

(above and opposite)

Nestled deep in the Big Thicket of East Texas is the state's oldest reservation, home to the 550 members of the Alabama-Coushatta Tribe of Texas. These Native Americans celebrate the traditions of their own proud heritage, while honoring their shared history with newer Texans. Tribe members have fought valiantly alongside of Texans during the Texas Revolution, the Civil War and World War II.

ASIAN MARKET, CHINATOWN *(top)*

GRILLED DOVE *(bottom)*

Many Chinese menus feature gourmet Peking
Duck. The main ingredient may be found
right in Houston, Texas at an Asian market,
located in one of Houston's two Chinatowns.

Chinatown markets are bustling places of
exotic sights, sounds and aromas, filled with
many culinary delights to thrill the most
discriminating palate—from dim sum and
dumplings, to grilled dove, Peking duck and
steeped, jasmine tea.

FARMERS' MARKET

Shoppers at Houston's farmers' markets find a delectable variety of fresh-from-the farm fruits, vegetables, pecans, honey, flowers and other local products. High quality is guaranteed, because Texas certifies its farmers' markets.

CABO RESTAURANT, DOWNTOWN

(above and opposite)

A giant, red saxophone, electronic music and
metallic palm trees create a tropical atmos-
phere with a Tex-Mex menu reminiscent of
the famous Mexican town of Cabo San Lucas.
This stylish eatery is a favorite with locals.

TEXAS GUANDI TEMPLE, TEMPLE
OF THE WARRIOR BUDDHIST

In tribute to answered prayers, a Vietnamese
couple built the Guandi Temple, the largest
of its kind in the United States. The temple
is dedicated to the Warrior god Guandi,
defender against evil and protector of truth.

CHINATOWN *(top and bottom)*

In the 1870's, 300 Chinese laborers came to Houston to work on the railroads. From these first immigrants, the Asian community took root in Houston. Today there are two Chinatowns in the city—the original one downtown, which contains several well-known restaurants, and the new and larger Chinatown located in the Bellaire suburb. Predominantly populated with Mandarin-speaking Chinese, it is also home to many Vietnamese and other Asian immigrants.

SHRIMP BOAT FLEET *(top)*

The Kemah Basin is home to an active shrimp boat fleet. The Annual Blessing of the Fleet and Boat Parade is held each August with crowds viewing from the shore as elaborately decorated boats pass by for their blessing.

TEXAS CHICKEN *(bottom)*

Texas Chicken is a game of bravado played when boat captains test their skills against each other in the narrow confines of the Houston Boat Channel. Each aims dead ahead, trying to intimidate the other captain into surrendering the right of way.

THE ELYSSA *(opposite)*

This majestic, tall ship with three masts, nineteen sails and an iron hull, was built in 1877 in Scotland. One of the grandest square-riggers of her day, the 205-foot historic landmark can be boarded at the Texas Seaport Museum.

CONTAINER TERMINAL *(top and bottom)*

The Port of Houston is one of the busiest ports in the country and handles more foreign tonnage than any other U.S. port. It handles its share of container shipping, but the largest volume of shipments in this gulf port is petrochemical and other bulk materials.

OIL TANKING *(opposite)*

Ships line up along Houston's Ship Channel, like cars at a gas station, to hook up to massive pipelines and fill their tanks with petroleum refined at the many petrochemical plants in the port area.

TUGS (top)

Tug boats are the hardest workers in the shipping channel, nudging and maneuvering massive barges, ships and tankers through the channel's hectic marine traffic to and from the safety of portside berths.

OIL TANKS (bottom)

In this crude-oil mecca, the strength and focus of the country's largest petrochemical complex is concentrated in Houston's Ship Channel, where over twenty petrochemical plants refine crude oil from far below the deep waters of the Gulf.

SUCCESS (opposite)

A crane on this off-shore oil platform delivers a piece of equipment that is used only when the drilling has successfully hit a gas deposit below the Gulf waters. Jobs on these rigs can include long days of intense heat, or crushing seas with hurricane force winds.

CO$_2$ FRAC PUMP

This type of off-shore drilling pump has
proven to be an economical and efficient way
to help extract oil and gas from the sandy
bottom of Gulf waters. At the same time, the
use of the CO$_2$ frac pump is environmentally
friendlier than other extraction techniques.

OFF SHORE DRILLING

The Ocean Star at Galveston's Pier 19 is a
museum, a hands-on education lab, and a
working drilling rig all rolled into one. It
clearly illustrates why Houston is the nation's
petroleum leader.

ROUGHNECKS OFFSHORE

Oil production and environmental issues may
come and go with the profits that these off-
shore rigs bring in for their companies. However, throughout all of the changes and advances
this industry has experienced over the last
century, one fact remains: it's a dirty business.

EXPANSION OF GEORGE R. BROWN CONVENTION CENTER *(top)*

The GRB Convention Center boasts 1.2 million square feet of meeting, exhibition and registration space. Under new expansion plans, the GRB will include a business center, visitors center and, of course, a Starbucks.

PUMP JACK ON GOLD COURSE *(bottom)*

In Houston, lining up your best shot on the 15th hole sometimes includes the phrase, *"to the left of the pump jack."* One of the newest golf courses in South Houston, Pump Jack, pays tribute to the area's rich history.

HOLOCAUST MUSEUM *(above)*

In March of 1996, the Holocaust Museum began educating people about the Holocaust and its six-million Jewish victims. The museum's mission also includes educating and heightening public awareness of genocide and human rights violations in the world today.

HOUSTON AQUARIUM *(opposite)*

Houston's amazing aquarium is a six-acre entertainment and dining complex centered around 200 species of exotic fish in one-half-million gallons of water. Located downtown, this popular attraction also has a bar, ballroom and plenty of exhibits.

NASA HOT AIR BALLOON FESTIVAL

Each year, on the last weekend of August, Texans across from Nassau Bay get sore necks when the Ballunar Liftoff Festival launches near Clear Lake at NASA's Johnson Space Center. This is one of the largest competitions in the country. Events test pilots' navigation and maneuvering skills. The festival features over a hundred spectacular balloons, along with powered flight vehicles of every description.

BALLUNAR LIFTOFF FESTIVAL

NASA'S Johnson Space Center opens it gates
to this family oriented event where the beauty
of massive hot air powered balloons are in
stark contrast to the high tech world of space
travel.

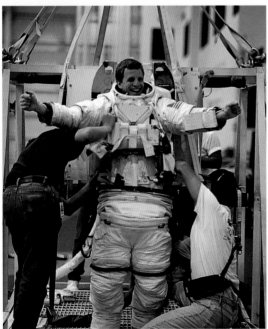

NASA MISSION CONTROL *(above and opposite)*

Nicknamed *Space City*, Houston is home to NASA's Johnson Space Center, easily the city's most popular tourist attraction. There is so much to do and see that you can easily spend the better part of a day here, immersed in the thrill of space exploration. Visit the Space Center for interactive displays and simulations of weightlessness, or take the tram tour to the real NASA control center where you might actually see astronauts in training.

HOUSTON TEXANS *(above)*

A young franchise, the Houston Texans have already shown that they can compete well in the NFL. Houstonians, who love their football as much as they love being Texans, are happy to have an NFL team after the departure of the Oilers in 1996.

MINUTE MAID PARK *(opposite, top and bottom)*

Minute Maid Park is one of the premier ballparks in baseball, though from the outside some worry that with its dome it looks like a football stadium. With roof retracted, the park provides unobstructed views of the nation's fourth largest city.

TRACKING HOME RUNS *(top)*

Minute Maid's outfield has a unique feature atop its cream-colored wall: a replica 1860's locomotive with a linked coal car on a railroad track. The coal car chugs down the track whenever a Houston Astros batter hits a home run.

RELIANT STADIUM *(bottom and opposite)*

When it opened in September 2002, Reliant Stadium was the first facility with a retractable roof of its kind in the NFL. This feature not only got Houston the Super Bowl in 2004, but it now hosts rodeos that draw over two million people every year.

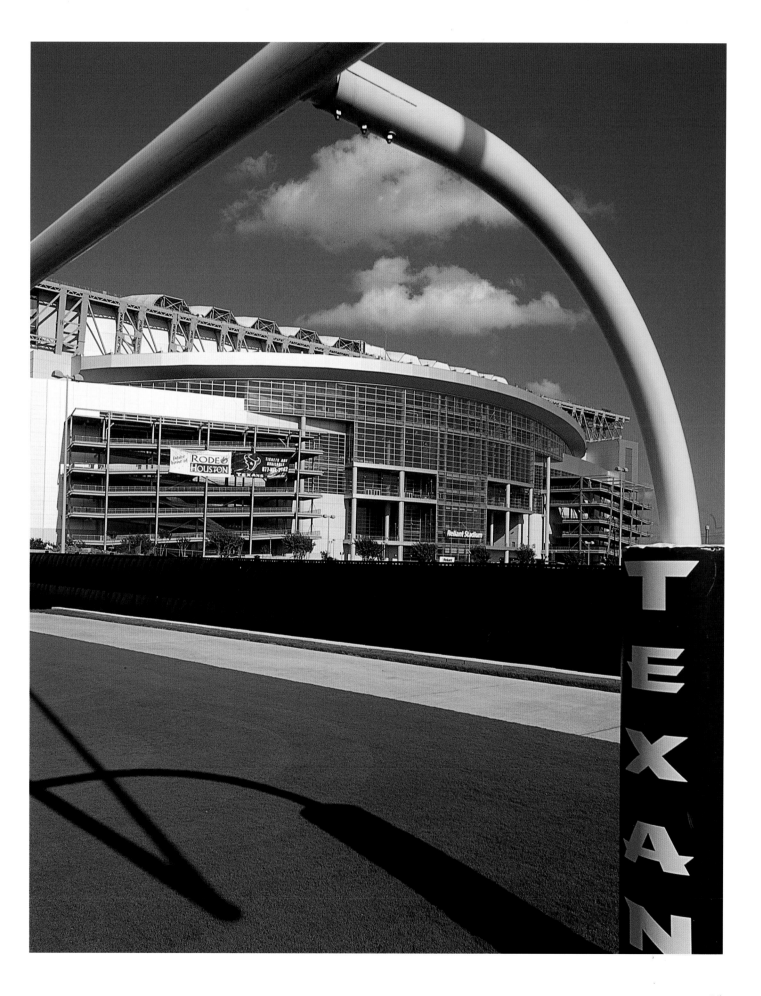

PICNIC LOOP BIKERS *(top)*

Memorial Park, the largest urban park in
Houston, is a favorite with bikers due to its
mile-long, bike path. On weekends and late
afternoons, numerous bikers pedal along
paved lanes that wind through the shaded
park for over a mile without car traffic.

BEACH RIDING, GALVESTON *(bottom)*

Galveston Island State Park is 2,000 acres
located on a barrier island. Two miles of
gulf-beach access is available, with picnic
spots, campsites for RVs, and four miles of
hiking and biking trails that wind among the
park's lakes and bayous.

SAM HOUSTON RACE PARK

Experience the excitement of real horsepower thundering around the track at this Class-A race park in northwest Houston. Thoroughbred racing fills the seats from November through April, and quarter-horse races thrill fans in the summer.

FATHER-SON TIME

A favorite get-away with city dwellers,
Galveston is known for its thirty-two miles
of beautiful, family-friendly beaches and
cool, gulf breezes. Since alcohol is not
allowed on the beach or in parks, this popular resort setting is safe and fun for everyone.

PELICANS ON GALVESTON ISLAND

Galveston Island offers excellent birding,
particularly on the bay side. Drawn by the
food-rich bayous and marshes, wading birds,
like the roseate spoonbill, white ibis, great
egret, great blue heron, gulls and pelicans,
can be sighted regularly.

FEATHERFEST

Featherfest is an annual birding and nature
festival that has been sponsored by The
Galveston Island Nature Tourism Council
since 2003. Its mission includes raising environmental awareness and increasing tourism.

COASTAL BIRDING, GALVESTON

Galveston sits astride a great birding migra-
tion route, and is close to other world-class
birding refuges. The festival has developed a
big following, according to its founders,
because of Galveston's unique ambience.

BRAZORIA NATIONAL WILDLIFE
REFUGE *(above)*

Created for migratory birds, this 40,000-acre
wetland refuge is home to more than 300
bird species, and over 200 exotic waterfowl
species that co-exist in a perfect mixture of
mudflats and marshes.

REDDISH EGRET *(opposite)*

Brazoria ranks first or second in the nation
for the variety of species sightings, according
to the National Audubon Society. With that
in mind, The Friends of Brazoria have
installed an automatic gate, which allows
access to the refuge from sunrise to sunset.

SWALLOW-TAIL BUTTERFLY, AREA
LAKE

Over 300 species make South Texas a premier
butterfly refuge. In addition, the diversity of
habitat in the lower Rio Grande has attracted
over 500 species of birds, including raptors,
neotropical migratory birds and shorebirds.

CYPRESS KNEES, WALLISVILLE
RESERVOIR

Bald cypress trees add an eerie and haunting
mood to the wetlands and swamps around
Houston. The trees' unusual stumps or *knees*
are growths that supply oxygen down into the
root system and help anchor the tree in its
unstable, watery environment. Bald cypress
trees can live for hundreds of years in their
fragile eco-system, providing a nesting place
for hawks, blue herons, turtles and snakes.

MUSEUM OF FINE ARTS *(top)*

The first art museum in Texas, the Museum of Fine Arts, is a cultural complex of artistic expression, including two museum buildings, two art schools, international traveling exhibits, a sculpture garden, and two decorative arts centers.

SESQUICENTENNIAL PARK *(opposite)*

Buffalo Bayou Sesquicentennial Park has become a splendid addition to Houston's Theatre District. Adjacent to the Wortham Theatre, the park, completed in 1989, includes a cascading fountain, gatehouse, and dramatic octagonal pavilion.

BAY FISHING (above and opposite)

Whether combining kayaking with bay fishing, or just wading out in hip-highs, the blue
gulf waters of the Texas coast are one of the
nation's prime destinations for angling and
sports fishing. Clear Lake and Galveston Bay
are also extremely popular for sailing. The
Bay Area Sailing Association holds sailing
workshops and hands-on classes for begin-
ners and more advanced sailors who want to
fine-tune their boating skills as the gulf
breezes fill their sales.

BLACKBERRIES FOR THE PICKING

Brazos blackberries are an erect, thorny fruit that were cultivated and released by the Texas Agricultural Experiment Station in 1959. High in acidity, brazos are used mostly for jams, jellies and baking. The crop is usually ripe for the picking in mid May. If you're in the mood, the Houston area has scores of beautiful "u pick 'em" farms to choose from, but be warned—the best berries are gone by noon.

BLUE BONNETS IN SPRING

In early spring, throughout central and
southern Texas, the huge flat plain ripples
in shimmering color. An extraordinary scene,
Texas is transformed into a French
Impressionist painting.

HOUSTON ZOO ENTRANCE

African Elephant, by Bob Fowler, has been standing at the west entrance to the zoo since 1982. Unlike the Asian elephant, it's the only elephant that can't be tamed and may become extinct in our lifetime.

MEMORIAL PARK

The largest urban park in Texas shares its name with a collection of residential neighborhoods. The area, just east of Loop 610 West, encompasses Crestwood, Camp Logan, Rice Military, and communities such as Arlington Court.

BUFFALO BAYOU HIKE & BIKE TRAIL

A top priority of the Buffalo Bayou Partner-
ship has been to build plentiful walking and
biking trails on the north and south banks of
Buffalo Bayou. This twenty-mile stretch of
perfect nature trails is a jewel in the middle
of downtown.

AERIAL VIEW OF HERMANN PARK

Hermann Park is Houston's most significant green space. Here, the Houston Zoo, Miller Outdoor Theatre, the Houston Museum of Natural Science, and the first desegregated golf course in the U.S, all add to its stature.

CINCO RANCH *(top)*

This is la dolce vita for some Houstonians. Cinco Ranch is a new, 7,400-acre, planned community that comes with cream-colored beaches and tree-lined jogging trails. Complete with clear blue water in a four-foot, swimming lagoon.

URBAN SPRAWL *(opposite)*

For those settled here, Houston has much to offer. Great schools, job opportunities, professional sports teams and a variety of cultural events are only some of the ammenities that make Houston a shining star on the beautiful Gulf Coast.

HOUSTON HEIGHTS *(above and opposite)*

Time seems to stand still in a community-oriented neighborhood called The Heights, north of downtown. Rooted in the late 1800's, Houston Heights has preserved many of the Victorian homes within its borders. Seasonal festivals throughout the year give locals and strangers alike a chance to revisit this American still-life. Marked with historical plaques, memorials to veterans and antique shops, The Heights conveys the warmth of Main Street USA.

TRAIL RIDING *(above)*

No single endeavor has branded the image of Texas in the national mind more than the cattle drive, even though most Texas herds ran only from the mid 1860's to the 1880's— before refrigeration made them obsolete.

GEORGE RANCH COWBOY *(opposite)*

Set on 23,000 acres of working ranch and farmland, the George Ranch Historical Park brings old Texas to life for visitors through authentic, historical settings. The ranch has become one of Houston's most popular heritage attractions.

TRAIL RIDING *(top and opposite)*

The George Ranch Historical Park holds
100 years of Texas' biggest stories, from
cattle and cotton to oil; from the Texas
revolution to taking down longhorns. Some
visitors enjoy the area's historical house tours,
or living history exhibits, while others simply
experience the Texas of the past by going on
a trail ride. The sights, smells, sounds and
tastes of a "Texas-that-was" make it easy to
leave the modern world behind.

HOUSTON RODEO *(above and opposite)*

Eagerly anticipated every year, this beloved
event is the largest rodeo and livestock show
on earth, as well as one of the world's largest,
most prestigious horse shows. The extravaganza attracts millions of fans to its nonstop
thrills.

DESPERADOS

Launching the three-week-long Houston Livestock Show and Rodeo is its most popular event: the Downtown Rodeo Parade. Drawing as many spectators as the rodeo itself, the parade has been growing in size since 1938. Today, thousands of men and women in wagons and on horseback—including civic leaders, performers, competitors, and entertainers—parade with marching bands and extravagant floats, kicking off the most anticipated event on the rodeo circuit.

ON A TRAIL RIDE

Nearly 4,800 cowboys and cowgirls saddle up with over 200 covered wagons on trail rides from as far as way as Hidalgo, Texas (386-miles) to relive the Old West on their way to the famous Houston Livestock Show and Rodeo.

BOOTS 'N BUTTS

Brave men with numbers on their backs ride ill-tempered bulls, bucking broncos and throw a lasso as needed. These are the stars of the American rodeo, though many are unknown outside of close circles, like most of the cowboy heroes that made Houston a great city. While dude ranches may cater to city slickers turned weekend cowboys, there are still working cattle drives throughout Texas that rely on the traditional "cowboy way" that has been so instrumental in the development of the American Southwest.